ALL
ABOUT
ME

My Feelings

CARYN JENNER

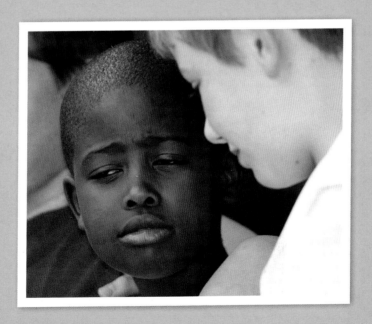

W

FRANKLIN WATTS
LONDON · SYDNEY

Franklin Watts
338 Euston Road
London NW1 3BH

Franklin Watts Australia
Level 17/207 Kent Street
Sydney, NSW 2000

Series editor: Sarah Peutrill
Art director: Jonathan Hair
Design: www.rawshock.co.uk
Picture researcher: Kathy Lockley
Consultant: Molly Wolfe,
Child Therapist

Many of the pictures is this book are posed
by models. All scenarios are fictitious and
any similarities to people, living or dead, are
purely coincidental.

Dewey number: 153

ISBN 978 1 4451 2975 4

Printed in China

Franklin Watts is a division of Hachette
Children's Books,
an Hachette UK company.
www.hachette.co.uk

Picture credits: Judy Barranco/iStockphoto:
24. Max Blain/Shutterstock: 6R. Mike Booth/
Alamy: 26. Bubbles Photolibrary/Alamy:
12, 16, 21. Laurent Davoust/iStockphoto:
7. Sheryl Griffin/iStockphoto: 19. Jeanne
Hatch/Shutterstock: 23B. interactimages/
Shutterstock: 10. Crystal Kirk/Shutterstock:
6L. Linda Kloosterhof/iStockphoto:
11T. Kevin Lepp/Shutterstock: 9. Sean
Locke/iStockphoto: 11B. Liza McCorkle/
iStockphoto: 8. mammamaart/iStockphoto:
27B. Patricia Marks/Shutterstock: cover,
20. Rob Marmion/Shutterstock: 14, 27T.
Gideon Mendel/Corbis: 13R. metrmetr/
Shutterstock: 15. Aldo Murillo/iStockphoto:
25B. Cliff Parnell/iStockphoto: Title page, 6C,
25T. Richard Schultz/Corbis: 23T. Dawna
Stafford/iStockphoto: 13L. vario images
GmbH & Co/Alamy: 18, 22. Janine Wiedel/
Photofusion: 17.

Every attempt has been made to clear
copyright. Should there be any inadvertent
omission please apply to the publisher for
rectification.

CONTENTS

(Words in **bold** are in the glossary on page 28.)

WHAT ARE FEELINGS?

How do you feel right now? Do you feel happy, sad, worried, shy, grumpy, angry, excited, scared, jealous, bored or confused? These are all feelings, describing your **mood**. Feelings are also known as **emotions**. In this book, we talk about some of the feelings that people have, but there are many more.

? Can you tell how each child might be feeling in these pictures?

EVERYONE HAS FEELINGS

You have feelings - and it's important to remember that everyone else does too. Adults have feelings, even parents and teachers. Some people show their feelings more than others. But we all have a whole range of feelings and it is helpful to give each one a name.

Sometimes, feelings are like the ups and downs of a rollercoaster ride.

CHANGING FEELINGS

It would be wonderful if we felt happy all the time. But how we feel can change, depending on the things we do, the thoughts we have and everything that happens around us. You can also have more than one feeling at the same time. For example, if you're planning a school trip away, you might feel excited, happy, worried and scared - all at the same time.

You can't **control** which feelings you have or when you have them. But what you *can* control is what you do about your feelings. For instance, if you feel happy, you'll probably want to smile!

BE AWARE OF YOUR FEELINGS

It helps to try to be **aware** of a feeling as it happens. One clue to how you feel on the inside is often the way that your feelings affect your body on the outside.

For example, your skin may tingle when you are excited, or your mouth may dry up if you feel **nervous**. If you take notice of how you feel, you'll have a better idea of what to do about it.

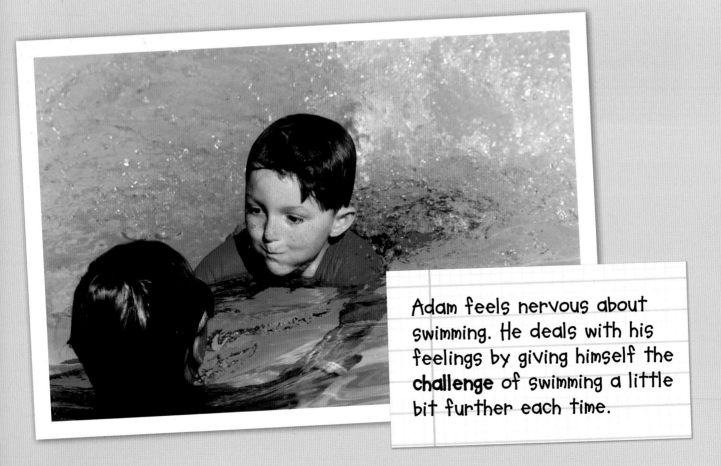

Adam feels nervous about swimming. He deals with his feelings by giving himself the **challenge** of swimming a little bit further each time.

TALKING ABOUT FEELINGS

At times, your feelings may seem to take over, making it hard to think straight. Telling someone else how you feel puts you back in charge of your feelings and makes them easier to deal with. By sharing your feelings with someone you **trust**, you'll get another point of view, and the comfort of someone who cares about you and how you feel.

Have you heard people say, "You'll feel better if you get it off your chest"? What they mean is that it helps to talk about your feelings.

When Jay's mum notices that he's feeling grumpy, she jokes with him until he can't help but laugh.

When you're feeling happy, you might be jumping up and down with excitement, or you might feel quietly content or something in between. When you're happy, you smile and laugh and you have more energy. It feels good!

Kimiko is happy playing with her friends.

HAPPINESS FROM INSIDE

Happiness often comes from sharing experiences with other people or from things that happen in your life. But happiness also comes from inside you. If you feel good about yourself, you'll feel happier.

Fred is happy being with his pet cat.

THINK POSITIVE

It's impossible to be happy all the time - but if you're happy most of the time, it helps to get you through the sad or worrying times. So think **positive** - hope for the best, but be prepared to change your plans if things don't go your way.

Jenny and her team are happy they've won the trophy!

What makes **you** feel happy? Write down your answers in a list and look at them whenever you're in need of a smile!

SAD

Imagine a black cloud above you, following wherever you go and pressing down on you. That is a bit like sadness. There are many reasons why you might feel sad. When you feel sad, you may feel like crying. Crying is okay - it's a way to let your feelings out.

Vicky feels sad because her gran died. She misses the chats she used to have with her gran.

DEEP SADNESS

You are likely to feel very sad if someone you love dies. You'll miss the person very much and it may feel like a big hole in your life. You may feel tired and lose interest in the things that you normally like. These feelings are **normal** and should fade over time. Remember that the person you miss would not want you to stay sad.

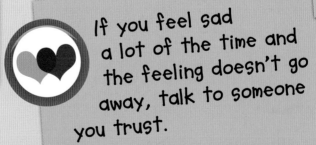

If you feel sad a lot of the time and the feeling doesn't go away, talk to someone you trust.

WHAT MAKES YOU SAD?

You might also feel sad if you are lonely, or if someone has said or done something to make you feel sad. Small things can make you feel a little sad, too. Perhaps you feel sad at the end of a holiday or if you can't play with your friend. This kind of sadness usually passes quickly and is soon forgotten.

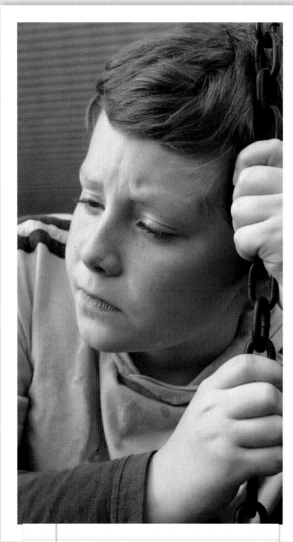

Liam feels sad because he has no one to play with. He is lonely.

Hanan feels sad because her best friend, Neela, has moved away. She talks to her teacher, who makes her feel better.

It's natural to feel worried sometimes. You might feel nervous, with a strange feeling called 'butterflies in your tummy', or you might even feel ill. When you worry, it's usually because you're not sure what will happen. But often the worries are worse than what actually happens.

WHEN WORRIES TAKE OVER

Some worries may seem to take over, especially if you feel you can't do anything about them. You might feel **anxious** about moving home, changes to your family or a visit to the doctor. Talk over your worries with someone you trust. You could also write your worries down or draw a picture if it's hard to find the right words. This might help you to think about your **concerns** more clearly.

Eliza is worried about moving to a new home. What will her new school be like? Will she make new friends? She talks to her mum about it while they pack.

Jordan is worried about a school project. Next time he won't leave it until the last minute – and then he won't be so worried!

EVERYDAY WORRIES

Do you find that you worry about lots of different things every day? Worries such as: Have you learnt your spellings well enough? Who will you play with at playtime? Will you like the school dinner today? Try not to let little worries become big worries.

WHEN WORRIES BECOME FEARS

Sometimes, you might be so worried that you become scared of trying new things. Think about things you've done that you are proud of. Don't let your fears stop you from trying and if you don't **succeed** first time - keep trying!

Close your eyes and imagine that your worries are bubbles in the air. In your mind, watch the bubbles float away, and imagine that these are your worries vanishing into the sky.

Everyone feels shy sometimes. You might want to raise your hand in class, join in a game or make a new friend, but you feel nervous. Your mind might go blank or you could feel hot or ill. Being shy is when you feel nervous with other people.

HAVE A GO!

It can be hard raising your hand or doing other things in front of people. But remember that they are interested in what you are saying or doing. Have a go! It gets easier the more you do it, and soon you won't be shy.

KEEP TRYING

In the past, you may have got an answer wrong so you might be scared of doing it again. But everyone makes mistakes so don't be hard on yourself. Remember, nobody's perfect. Just try again.

Karl thinks he knows the answer to the question, so he raises his hand even though he feels shy.

Izzy feels shy as she watches the group of children. She takes a deep breath, ready to smile and join them.

MAKING FRIENDS

Remember the special reasons others would want to be friends with you - perhaps you're kind or you know lots of good jokes! Try to find out what you have in common with other people. Look at them and smile and they're likely to smile back. At playtimes, ask other children if they want to play. If they say no, it doesn't mean they don't want to be your friend. It probably just means they're already busy.

Think about things you can talk about when making new friends, such as: "What have you got for lunch today?" or "You're brilliant at skipping. Can you teach me?"

If you feel shy about doing something, how can you boost your **confidence?**'

GRUMPY

Has anyone ever asked you if you've woken up on the wrong side of the bed? What they mean is that you seem to be in a grumpy mood. Everything seems to be annoying you and you take it out on the people around you.

Sadie doesn't feel like playing with her friends today. She's too grumpy.

A GRUMPY MOOD

Grumpy moods are puzzling - often you don't know why you feel this way. Was it because of bad weather or because you ran out of your favourite breakfast cereal? Once a grumpy mood strikes, it feels like the entire day will be a disaster. You might find yourself being cheeky to your mum, snapping at your best friends or frowning at your teacher. You can't seem to help it.

You are more likely to feel grumpy if you are tired or hungry. So get plenty of sleep and eat healthy foods, especially at breakfast.

FEELING BETTER

Look around you and see how much fun you are missing as a result of your grumpy mood. You might just need a few minutes alone to talk to yourself. Set yourself a challenge - try to smile, even if you don't feel like it. Look at the list of things that makes you happy (page 11). Does it turn your frown into a smile?

Quinn realises that his grumpy mood is ruining his fun with his dad. What can he and his dad do to cheer him up?

ANGRY

When you're angry, it's hard to deal with your feelings. Anger is natural, but everyone must learn to control it, so that no one gets hurt. Once you calm down, you can think more clearly and people are more likely to listen to what you have to say.

HOW DOES ANGER FEEL?

You might feel angry if someone hurts you. You might even get angry because someone else is angry! When you're angry, your heart races, you breathe quickly and you might clench your fists tightly.

If Patrick and Sasha would calm down and control their anger, they could sort out their differences.

CONTROLLING YOUR ANGER

If you're angry, give your brain time to think. Walk away if you can, at least for a few moments to calm down. Then you can think about how to deal with the problem. You might even decide it's not worth getting angry about, or you might find a way to work it out by talking the problem through.

TEMPER TANTRUMS

Some people get angry and have temper tantrums if they don't get their own way. You've probably seen small children shouting and stamping their feet. It looks a bit silly, doesn't it? Small children have tantrums because they haven't learned to control their anger, and they may not have the words yet to tell people why they're angry.

CALM WORDS

You can **express** yourself though, so calm words are the best way to get your point across. But even so, don't expect to get your own way every time.

Natalia is angry because she thinks her mum isn't being fair. She takes a deep breath to calm down before telling her mum how she feels.

Ideas for calming anger:
- Breathe deeply.
- Walk away until you are calm.
- Count to ten slowly (or higher!).
- Repeat to yourself, 'Be calm. I CAN handle this.'

- Tell someone else how you feel.
- Use up angry energy with exercise.
- If you've fallen out with someone, try to sort it out by talking – not shouting!

It's not fair! How often do you think this? Everyone does at one time or another. You see what another person has and you want it for yourself. This can make you jealous. But things cannot always be fair for everyone.

WHY NOT ME?

You might feel jealous of a friend's new bike or of a classmate who's chosen for the school football team. It's not easy, but try to be happy for other people. Feeling jealous will make you feel bad: why are they so lucky and not you? Sometimes, jealousy can make you try harder. For instance, if you're jealous when your friend earns extra playtime for good behaviour, you might try to earn extra playtime too.

Sonya's friend, Flora, is playing with someone else today. They asked Sonya if she wants to join in, but she is too jealous.

Elinor feels jealous that her mum is playing with her sister. But Elinor's had her turn and she knows she has to learn to share.

BROTHERS AND SISTERS

It's normal to feel jealous of your brothers or sisters sometimes. After all, you've got to share so many things - including your parents' attention. It may hurt when you see them praising your brother or sister or spending time with them. But sometimes it's *you* who gets praise and attention, and your brothers and sisters might be jealous.

Babies need lots of attention, so it's easy to be jealous when a new baby joins the family. How would you deal with jealous feelings if you had a new baby in your family?

It's good to be aware of other people's feelings, as well as your own. Noticing how other people feel is part of what makes a nice person and a good friend.

When the older girls saw Claire sitting by herself on the school bus, they realised she was worried about her first day at school. They made friends with her, and now Claire is happy to be starting school.

CLUES TO FEELINGS

People don't always come right out and say how they are feeling. But you can get clues from the look on people's faces, their tone of voice or how they act. For example, if your friend is frowning and doesn't join in at playtime that might be a clue that your friend is feeling sad, worried, shy or lonely. But don't demand to know what it wrong. That often makes people feel worse. Instead, gently say that if he or she needs a friend to talk to, you would like to help.

LISTENING AND CARING

If someone trusts you with their feelings, then you should pay attention and listen. Helping someone doesn't always mean giving advice or trying to find solutions. Just listening may be enough. It means that you care, and sometimes that's all a person needs to start feeling a bit better.

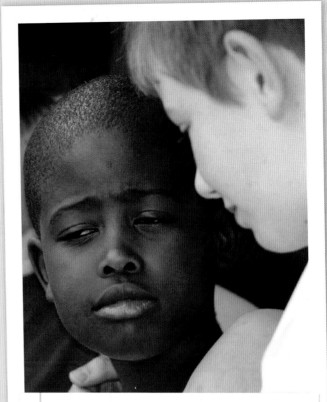

Jason listens to Calvin talk about how sad he feels that his dog died. It makes Jason feel sad too, but he's glad to help his friend.

Make sure to share happy feelings as well! Zara's mum is very excited to talk about her new job. Zara tells her mum that she's really happy for her.

People often want to keep their feelings **private**, so be careful who else you tell. But if the problem is too big to handle, tell an adult that you trust or phone the Childline hotline (see page 29).

It's no fun feeling sad or grumpy or angry. Feeling happy and feeling good about ourselves is what we all want. So, what makes you feel good? Here are a few ideas.

BE THE BEST YOU CAN BE

Being the best you can be means trying your hardest. It doesn't mean comparing yourself to other people because everyone is different. And it doesn't mean you should expect to be perfect because nobody is perfect. But it does mean you should try your best and keep on trying. It's not always easy, but you'll get a great feeling of pride and satisfaction.

BE KIND

Be kind to others. When you make other people feel good, you make yourself feel good too. It's a brilliant feeling to see someone smile and know that *you* helped to make that person happy. Be kind to yourself as well. Spend time doing interesting things. Find a hobby that you enjoy, or try something you've never done before. It might just be fun!

It took her a long time to learn, but now Orla is a great hula-hooper and she feels proud that she finally did it!

Sam shows Chloe how to get started on a homework task. He is glad that he can help.

LAUGH A LOT!

There's a saying that laughter is the best medicine. In fact, when you laugh, your body sends feel-good chemicals to your brain. Some doctors even say that laughter makes you healthier. So go on - have a giggle or a chuckle, or a great big belly laugh and see how good it makes you feel!

Matt and his brother Finlay get a fit of the giggles. Laughing makes them feel good – which is lucky becomes sometimes they can't stop!

Anxious to feel especially worried or scared about something

Aware knowing about something, for example, being aware of your feelings means knowing that they are there

Challenge a competition or test, especially to test yourself

Concerns worries

Confidence believing in yourself, for example, believing that you can do something

Control to have power over something in order to deal with it

Emotions feelings

Express to communicate something, for example, to say or show how you feel

Mood how you feel

Nervous to feel a little worried

Normal natural, not unusual

Positive to be hopeful and think good things

Private something that you do not want to share with other people

Succeed to do well at something, achieve a goal

Trust to believe in someone or something. Someone you trust should care about you and be willing to help you.

Websites

Childline - counselling service for children and young people.
Freephone: 0800 1111
www.childline.org.uk

Kidscape - preventing bullying, protecting children
www.kidscape.org.uk

Family Links - transforming schools and families
www.familylinks.org.uk

The Place 2 Be - school-based counselling service, dedicated to improving the emotional wellbeing of children, their families and the whole school community.
www.theplace2be.org.uk

Note to parents and teachers: Every effort has been made by the Publishers to ensure that these websites are suitable for children, that they are of the highest educational value, and that they contain no inappropriate or offensive material. However, because of the nature of the Internet, it is impossible to guarantee that the contents of these sites will not be altered. We strongly advise that Internet access is supervised by a responsible adult.

Books

Michael Rosen's Sad Book by Michael Rosen and Quentin Blake (Walker Books)

The Huge Bag of Worries by Virginia Ironside and Frank Rodgers (Hodder)

A Volcano in My Tummy: Helping Children to Handle Anger by Elaine Whitehouse and Warwick Pudney (New Society Publishers)

All by Margot Sunderland, (Speechmark Publishing):
A Nifflenoo Called Nevermind (A Story for Children Who Bottle Up Their Feelings)
Teeny Weeny in a Too Big World (A Story for Fearful Children)
Ruby and the Rubbish Bin (A Story for Children with Low Self-Esteem)

'Your Emotions' series by Brian Moses and Mike Gordon (Wayland)

INDEX